KU-342-512

PAMPHLETS ON AMERICAN WRITERS • NUMBER 76

UNIVERSITY OF MINNESOTA

Stephen Crane

BY JEAN CAZEMAJOU

UNIVERSITY OF MINNESOTA PRESS • MINNEAPOLIS

92 856

813.4
CAZ

© Copyright 1969 by the University of Minnesota

ALL RIGHTS RESERVED

Printed in the United States of America at
Jones Press, Minneapolis

Library of Congress Catalog Card Number: 74-625287

PUBLISHED IN GREAT BRITAIN, INDIA, AND PAKISTAN BY THE OXFORD UNIVERSITY PRESS, LONDON, BOMBAY, AND KARACHI, AND IN CANADA BY THE COPP CLARK PUBLISHING CO. LIMITED, TORONTO

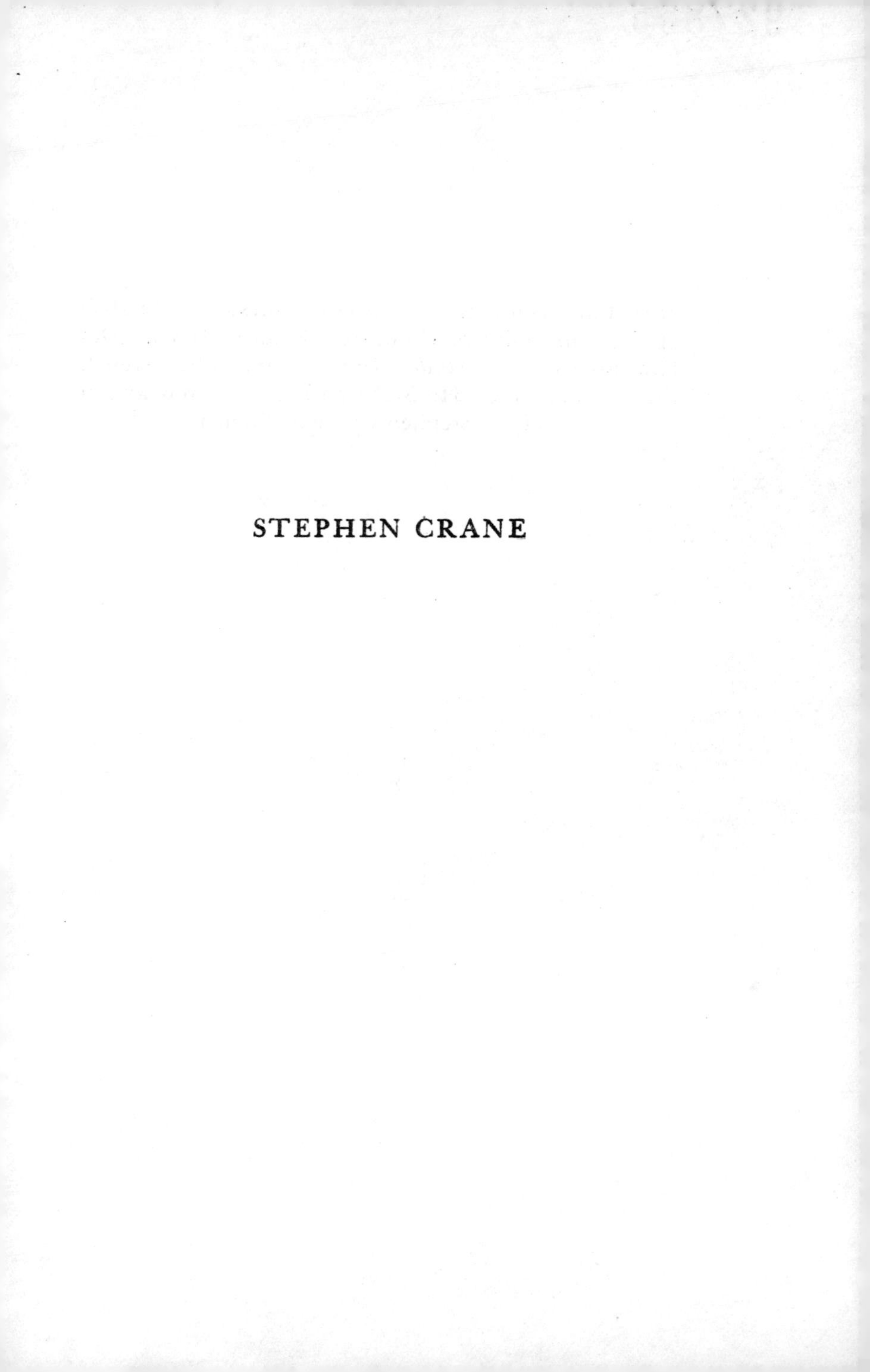

STEPHEN CRANE

JEAN CAZEMAJOU is an associate professor of English at the University of Bordeaux (France). His articles have appeared in *Etudes Anglaises* and other French literary magazines. He is the author of a book-length study of Stephen Crane in French.

Stephen Crane

Some writers work their way up to popularity in a long and difficult climb; others hit upon success almost overnight. Stephen Crane's second attempt at literary creation, his novel *The Red Badge of Courage*, met with triumphal acclaim early in 1896, but he lived long enough to enjoy only a few years of controversial fame.

Experimenting in various media – journalism, fiction, poetry, play writing – Crane was for his contemporaries above all a picturesque figure of the world of the press. His professional commitments kept him in close touch with the life of his country, and he explored slums and battlefields with unabating eagerness, seeing war in two brief conflicts in 1897 and 1898. The conjunction of highstrung temperament and obstinate neglect of his health brought Crane's life to an early close when he was not yet twenty-nine.

During the two decades following his death, in 1900, he was to be almost forgotten. Then in 1923 Thomas Beer published an impressionistic biography which served to focus attention on Crane once more, and *The Work of Stephen Crane* (1925–27), edited by Wilson Follett, made most of his writings available to a scholarly audience. This limited edition contained laudatory prefaces by creative writers such as Amy Lowell, Sherwood Anderson, H. L. Mencken, and Willa Cather, a few assessments by professional critics, and reminiscences by fellow journalists. Crane's reputation was also enhanced by the faithful support of some of his friends, especially Edward Garnett, Joseph Conrad, H. G. Wells, and Ford Madox Hueffer, later known as Ford

Madox Ford. The thirties saw in him a champion of the cause of the common man, and the forties continued to fit him into a realistic tradition; in the next two decades he has appeared to critics primarily as a symbolist, but a wide range of interpretations has confronted the student with a mass of conflicting scholarship. In 1950 John Berryman's *Stephen Crane* established him as an American classic. The Modern Library edition of *The Red Badge of Courage* came out the following year with a preface written by R. W. Stallman, whose extensive work on Crane, climaxed by his monumental biography in 1968, has aroused much enthusiasm and controversy. D. G. Hoffman's *The Poetry of Stephen Crane,* a very lively and perceptive study, appeared in 1957. Since 1951 there has also been a steady outpouring of articles, dissertations, monographs, and reprints. When, in the summer of 1966, a *Stephen Crane Newsletter* was founded and began to be issued regularly by Ohio State University, Stephen Crane had come into his own.

Stephen Crane had deep roots in the soil of New Jersey and was extremely proud of his American heritage. One of his ancestors bearing the same name had, according to Crane, "arrived in Massachusetts from England in 1635." The man who wrote *The Red Badge of Courage* was, on his father's side, descended from a long line of sheriffs, judges, and farmers, and another Stephen Crane had been one of the leading patriots of New Jersey during the Revolution; in his mother's family, as he humorously put it, "everybody, as soon as he could walk, became a Methodist clergyman — of the old, ambling-nag, saddle-bag, exhorting kind."

Born in a Methodist parsonage in Newark, New Jersey, on November 1, 1871, Stephen was the fourteenth child of Jonathan Townley Crane, D.D. He grew up in various parsonages in New Jersey and New York State, his father being, according to the custom of his church, shifted from one charge to another every two or three years. The death of Dr. Crane in Port Jervis, New York, in 1880 brought this itinerancy to a close. Still a child when his father died, Stephen always cherished his memory.

After the death of her husband Mrs. Crane returned to Newark for a while, but soon made a permanent home in Asbury Park, New Jersey, which was a new stronghold of American Methodism. There she settled in 1883 and, that same year, was elected president of the Woman's Christian Temperance Union of Asbury Park and Ocean Grove. Frequently lecturing in neighboring towns, she occasionally traveled to distant cities as a delegate of that organization. A well-educated woman, she also dabbled in journalism to eke out her meager resources and reported on the summer religious meetings on the New Jersey shore, contributing mostly to the *New York Tribune* and the *Philadelphia Press*. She suffered from mental illness for some months in 1886 and was to die in 1891. Her religious zeal did not inspire a similar response in Stephen and he left the fold of the church; but he remained dominated by fundamental religious precepts and patterns — charity, fraternity, redemption, and rescue — which he usually kept at an earthly level.

At the age of fourteen he left Asbury Park to go to the Pennington Seminary, a Methodist academy in New Jersey, and thus attended a school over which his father had ruled for ten years (1849–58). He did not complete the four-year course there but transferred in the middle of the third year to Claverack College and Hudson River Institute, a semi-military Methodist school near Hudson, New York. He stayed there from January 1888 to June 1890. His university education lasted only one year: it began at Lafayette College, a Presbyterian institution at Easton, Pennsylvania, where he spent the autumn term of 1890, and ended at Syracuse University the following June. All these schools stressed religious and classical studies and at no time did the young man feel any sympathy for these two branches of knowledge. He was already a rebel resolutely hostile to formal education and preferred to study "humanity."

Crane suffered both from his mother's moral severity and from her physical neglect of him, but in Asbury Park he enjoyed a happy freedom near the "soft booming sound of surf." The deaths of his father, his sister Agnes, his brother Luther, and finally his mother must have made his childhood and adolescence a period of many severe trials. Three of his older brothers played the part of father-substitutes, offering either material assistance or a questionable but attractive model. William, who became a lawyer in Port Jervis in 1881, and Edmund, a man of limited education but of generous heart who, in 1894, settled at Hartwood, near Port Jervis, often helped the young man in his financial difficulties at the beginning of his literary career. Jonathan Townley Jr.'s bohemian tastes exerted a powerful influence on his younger brother; almost twenty years older than Stephen, he was in the late 1880's the coast correspondent of the *New York Sun*, the *New York Tribune*, and the Associated Press in Asbury Park and so a well-known regional journalist. Stephen, as early as 1888, began helping him in his reportorial work on the New Jersey shore. His oldest sister, Nellie, who then kept an art school in Asbury Park, may have introduced Stephen to the world of color and prepared him for an aesthetic exploration of his environment.

Stephen Crane's sensitivity was thus early aroused and developed through a gradual training of his faculty of observation: Methodism forced him to probe his own soul, journalism taught him how to note facts with accuracy, and art provided his craving for reality with chromatic patterns.

After publishing a few pieces in *Cosmopolitan* and the *New*

York Tribune, a paper for which he wrote his "Sullivan County Sketches," boyish tales of the woods, in the early part of 1892, he was fired by the *Tribune* for an ironic article about a parade of workers in Asbury Park, and became a free-lance journalist in New York. (This brief report had expressed, in the tone of a sententious aesthete, his mild amusement at the sight of "an uncut and uncarved procession" of men with "principles" marching past a "decorous" throng of "summer gowns" and predatory Asbury Parkers.) Then began his apprenticeship in bohemianism in the metropolis, where he lived with struggling young artists. Occasional visits to his brothers Edmund and William helped him keep from starving; they provided him with handy refuges where he could escape from the hardships and turmoil of New York. His pride, however, prevented him from making frequent use of them. In 1893 he published his first book, *Maggie: A Girl of the Streets,* under a pseudonym and at his own expense. The audacity of the subject did not deter Hamlin Garland and W. D. Howells from praising that novel, but they were almost the only critics to notice it. They both encouraged him to write proletarian sketches, some of which appeared in the Boston *Arena* and others in the *New York Press,* enabling him to attain some financial security. His picture of the big city was centered around the life of the underprivileged in their ordinary setting, the southern tip of Manhattan.

Gradually acquiring self-reliance, experience, and ambition, he immersed himself in the most significant venture of his literary life, the writing of *The Red Badge of Courage,* an imaginative reconstruction of a Civil War battle; it was first printed in an abbreviated form as a newspaper serial distributed by the Bacheller Syndicate in December 1894. The success of the story led to an assignment as roving reporter in the West and Mexico at the beginning of 1895. When he came back in May, his first volume of verse, *The Black Riders,* had just appeared in print and proved that the young man was impelled by the spirit of religious and social rebellion. Appleton published *The Red Badge* as a book in New York in October 1895, and the London firm of Heinemann included it in its Pioneer Series at the end of November. Warmly received by English reviewers, it soon became a popular novel in the United States as well and its tenth American edition was issued in June 1896.

In that year Crane's celebrity reached a peak. All at once praised, parodied, and harshly criticized, he found it difficult to cope with success. Going from one apartment to another in New York and probably from one girl to another, he ended up challenging the impregnable metropolitan police force on behalf of a prostitute who claimed she was being unjustly harassed. Then, rushing into escape, he accepted a commission to report the insurrection in Cuba against Spanish rule, but his ship sank off the coast of Florida on January 2, 1897, and he returned to Jacksonville, where before sailing he had met Cora Howorth (known there as Cora Taylor), the proprietress of the Hotel de Dream, a somewhat refined house of ill-fame. She had already been married twice and, at the time of her first meeting with Crane, was thirty-one years old. They were to live together for the rest of his life. His previous adventures with women had been inconclusive episodes. At the age of twenty he had fallen in love, at Avon-by-the-Sea, a resort near Asbury Park, with a certain Helen Trent, who was already engaged. In 1892 a love affair with a young married woman, Lily Brandon Munroe, enlivened his summer in Asbury Park and inspired some of his more moving love letters. Nellie Crouse, a provincial maiden whom he met at a social tea in New York, flirted with him by mail but finally rejected him. In 1896 he started sending money to Amy Leslie, a former actress now past her prime who had become a drama critic for the *Chicago*

Daily News. He kept doing so until January 1898, when she succeeded in having a warrant of attachment issued against him to recover $550 of the $800 she had allegedly given him in 1896 to deposit for her. The details of their relationship remain somewhat obscure but, in November 1896, when he set out for Florida, he was probably fleeing from her as well as the New York police.

The year 1896 was not marked by any really new work from his pen, except his "Tenderloin" sketches for the *New York Journal*: Crane was too busy with his public and private life. *Maggie,* made respectable by the success of *The Red Badge* and slightly revised, came out under his real name, accompanied by another tale of the slums, *George's Mother,* which had been completed in November 1894. A volume of war stories, *The Little Regiment,* appeared in New York late in 1896 and in London in February 1897.

Crane's longing for adventure had apparently been only whetted by the shipwreck off Florida, in which he nearly lost his life; periodically the urge to see violent action was aroused in him. The Greco-Turkish War, which he covered in a disappointing manner for the *New York Journal* and the *Westminster Gazette,* took him to Europe in the summer of 1897; his bad health interfered with his reportorial duties in Greece, but he saw enough fighting to conclude on his return to London that "*The Red Badge* [was] all right."

Obviously conscious of the impossibility of introducing his "wife" — there is no record of a marriage ceremony — to his family, and still afraid of retaliatory action by the New York police, he decided to stay on in England after the Greek war was over. His shipwreck had inspired him to write a brilliant short story, "The Open Boat," which *Scribner's* printed in June 1897. About the same time he published *The Third Violet,* a novel based on his experiences in the highly contrasted worlds of Hartwood,

New York, and New York City. Crane's stay in England did not provide the writer with a fresh batch of literary topics but it did enable him to see his own life in a new perspective. Many of his western adventures and several accounts of urban poverty went into a volume published in 1898 under the title *The Open Boat and Other Tales of Adventure.* This volume, which contains seventeen tales, gives a sample of Crane's best talent. His meeting with Joseph Conrad brought him into contact with a writer whose aesthetics was very close to his own. In his "villa," situated on the borderline between Oxted and Limpsfield, Surrey, where he settled in the fall of 1897, Crane was not far from Ford Madox Hueffer and Harold Frederic. A few English Fabians, the Sydney Oliviers and the Edward Garnetts notably, lived in the vicinity.

In 1898 he was hired by Pulitzer to write for the *New York World* and, seeing war for the second time, reported the Spanish-American conflict, which left deep scars on his body and mind; the symptoms of the tuberculosis that was to prove fatal had already set in. In the fall he lingered in Havana where he served as special correspondent for the *New York Journal* and wrote the first draft of a novel, *Active Service,* based on his Greek assignment.

Early in 1899 he was back in England and, because of harassing creditors in Oxted, decided to move from Surrey to Sussex, his new English residence being the medieval manor of Brede Place situated near Rye on the charming Sussex coast. There his literary production reached a peak, but his efforts to avoid bankruptcy proved vain in the face of a rising tide of debts and recurring signs of failing health. He kept writing doggedly, now coaxing, now threatening his literary agent, James B. Pinker, from whom he tried to obtain more and more advances, and even the best work of this period shows the effects of haste and worry. Drawing upon his recent experiences, he completed a series of eleven fictional and autobiographical accounts of the Cuban war, which were posthumously collected in *Wounds in the Rain* (1900). He also wrote thirteen children's stories which first appeared in *Harper's Magazine* and were assembled in book form after his death under the title *Whilomville Stories* (1900). In the course of 1899 three other books saw print: a volume of verse, *War Is Kind,* containing a variety of poems whose composition embraced a period of seven years; *Active Service,* a novel which he himself regarded as second-rate; and the American edition of *The Monster and Other Stories.* Reminiscing about his family's role during the Revolutionary War, he composed three "Wyoming Valley Tales" and, creating an imaginary country, chose it as the setting for a series of archetypal battles, the "Spitzbergen Tales," which began to appear in English and American magazines in 1900.

Taking a mild interest in Cora's passion for entertaining, he watched streams of guests come to visit him in his dilapidated mansion, among whom were some distinguished writers (Conrad, Wells, Henry James) and many parasites. He decided or was persuaded by Cora to arrange a Christmas party for his literary friends, producing an original play for the occasion. The play was very aptly called *The Ghost* and, in spite of a widely advertised collaboration with famous English and American authors, most of it was written by Crane himself. During the festivities he almost died of a lung hemorrhage. He was to drag on for a few more months, his body and his brain gradually weakening, but he went on writing to his deathbed. With the help of Kate Lyon, Harold Frederic's mistress, he turned out a series of articles on nine great battles of the world for *Lippincott's Magazine,* outlined the plot and wrote the first twenty-five chapters of *The O'Ruddy,* a picaresque novel of the eighteenth century with an Irish hero and an English setting. But it was left uncompleted when Crane died on June 5, 1900, in Badenweiler, Germany, where Cora had seen fit to take him in the idle hope of a miraculous recovery from tuberculosis. Crane's friend Robert Barr agreed to write the final chapters of the novel which, after picaresque ups and downs, was eventually published in New York in October 1903.

The inescapable trait of Crane as a writer is his desire to express his own mind candidly, regardless of accepted opinion, conventions, and satirical attacks. The world first appeared to him with the colors, shapes, and sounds of the Psalms and of Wesleyan hymns, and he unconsciously made frequent use of the rhythms and imagery of Biblical stories. His parents' participation in charitable work encouraged his interest in slum life, and he soon discovered, through his own deep concern with the mainsprings of fear, a strange curiosity about war.

In Crane's generation "low life" was a subject of reportage, fiction, and melodrama. When he moved into this area of literature he did so with the seriousness, the intentness, and the acuteness of a minister's son who had received his training as a journalist. Even if he did not know New York well at the time he wrote *Maggie*, he must have caught by then a few glimpses of the poorer districts of the American metropolis, which was so close to Asbury Park where he lived between his stays at boarding school or college.

The approach to slum life of Crane's first novel was new in that it did not preach and did not encourage "slumming"; it simply aimed, he said, to "show people to people as they seem[ed] to [him]." Maggie is the daughter of the Johnsons, a family of poor tenement dwellers living on the lower East Side of Manhattan. A large part of the story is devoted to drinking bouts, and Maggie's home is the scene of a daily fight for survival. We thus attend the growth and brutal extinction of the heroine who has "blossomed in a mud-puddle" to become "a pretty girl" strangely undefiled by her surroundings. She tries to escape the degrading atmosphere of her home by working in a collar-and-cuff factory, but soon discovers the dull routine and corruption of the sweat-shop. Then Pete, a commonplace bartender, comes into her life, and to Maggie he seems to be "a supreme warrior," "a knight." He takes her to dime museums, beer gardens, and theaters, and thus satisfies her vague and romantic longings for culture and refinement. Seduced and abandoned by her lover, rejected by her drinking mother and callous brother on "moralistic" grounds, Maggie finally turns to prostitution. Shortly afterwards, "upon a wet evening," she abruptly ends her life in the East River while in the distance "street-car bells [jingle] with a sound of merriment."

The problem this story hinges on is not primarily a social one, and Crane is not merely content with studying the causes and consequences of prostitution. Mainly concerned with the "soul" of the young prostitute, he tries to challenge the beliefs of Sunday school religion. Can an "occasional street girl" be expected to end up in Heaven, irrespective of the indignant frowns of "many excellent people"? The answer is never made explicit in a narrative brimming over with irony, but it could not be other than positive. Maggie falls because "environment is a tremendous thing in the world," because she herself is romantic and weak, and also because nobody is interested in her fate. She, however, redeems herself by committing suicide, her only possible escape from a life of moral degradation. By so doing she undergoes an ironic purification in the foul waters of the East River while her brother Jimmie, who had "clad his soul in armour," and her mother who belatedly "ferg[ave]" her, are allowed to continue their degenerate lives of vice and hypocrisy in the human jungle to which they are perfectly adapted.

As a first novel *Maggie* revealed on the part of the author a deep seriousness and the powerful urge to gain an audience. It posited the imperative need for a new ethical code and, through a consistent use of irony, debunked the false values worshiped by society and exposed the part played by collective passivity in the destruction of innocence. "Indifference is a militant thing," Crane commented in a story of 1897; this idea is implied throughout *Maggie*. Much of this early Crane is reminiscent of the young Zola's passion for social rescue which found its most moving expression in *La Confession de Claude* (1865). The critics who wonder whether *Maggie* should be called a tragedy or a melodrama raise a fruitless issue, because the book is undeniably filled with pity and fear, and Howells was right when he discovered in it "that quality of fatal necessity which dominates Greek tragedy."

George's Mother is a companion piece to the drama of the New York prostitute, and it takes up again the problem of the corruption of innocence, this time in the person of a young workingman, George, who has recently settled in New York and lives in a tenement with his widowed mother, a very religious woman. The path leading to George's physical and moral destruction opens early in the story when he meets a former acquaintance, a certain Jones who introduces him into a circle of alcoholics. He thus misses work one day and invents a lie as an excuse for his absence. His mother, who tries to keep him from drifting, induces him to go with her to a prayer meeting which only "prov[es] to him again that he [is] damned." Plunging more resolutely into drink and dissipation, the young man inflicts great moral torture upon his mother who finally dies, worn down by disappointed expectations. The last scene shows her in the grips of her death agony, while her son, hastily called to her bedside, suddenly feels "hideous crabs crawling upon his brain." This book shows more interest in abstract ideas than in real people; it demonstrates the baneful effects of Sunday school religion upon George, who seeks refuge from it in drink, and the failure of this primitive faith to succor the mother in her sorest need. It also points to the impossibility of communication between human beings. The power corruptive influences and environment exert on immature minds is here again illustrated. This rather flimsy novel raises a number of issues but solves none and throughout are heard distinct echoes of Crane's conflict with his own mother.

The confined world of *George's Mother* could easily be contrasted with the maelstrom of life in Crane's New York City sketches, which he ranked among his "best work." He started his field study in the poorer districts of southern Manhattan, observing the motley streams of passers-by on Broadway, breadlines, crowds gathering outside cheap lodging houses, jingling streetcars, fires, Italian fruit-vendors, tramps, policemen, and here and there his camera eye stopped on a detail, a "tiny old lady" lost in "the tempest of Sixth Avenue," or two children fighting for a toy. His sympathy drew him instinctively to the cause of the common man, but he was more inclined to study the actual working of minds than the possible consequences of economic systems. In his study of the "Tenderloin," undertaken for the *New York Journal* in 1896, he calls up a picture of restaurants, dance halls, and opium dens where, beneath the superficial gaiety, slumbers the fire of an ever-present violence.

His technique in these city sketches follows three main patterns: that of the journey of initiation, exemplified by "An Experiment in Misery" and "An Ominous Baby"; that of canvas painting, in "The Men in the Storm," "An Eloquence of Grief," and "The Auction"; and that of the parody, in some of his "Tenderloin" stories. The reporter-errant selects a certain situation which becomes a pretext for a psychological study of urban conflicts. To him "the sense of city [was] battle."

How did Crane's war novel, *The Red Badge of Courage*, come into being against this background of urban literature? The book is not an ordinary Civil War novel. Although the theme is the baptism of fire of a Union private, Henry Fleming, during the battle of Chancellorsville, the tone is psychological rather than military. Its main characters are most of the time designated as figures in an allegory, "the tall soldier," "the loud soldier," "the tattered man," "the man of the cheery voice"; and the protagonist, usually referred to as "the youth" in the early chapters, only acquires his full identity in Chapter XI.

The author's observation of "the nervous system under fire" is conducted on the level of Henry's restless mind; before the battle we witness the premonitory misgivings of this farm boy in uniform; then comes his moment of reassurance after a first onslaught of the enemy has been repulsed. A second attack launched against his side causes his sudden panic and flight. Driven by shame to wander on the fringe of the battlefield, he seems to be helplessly floating in a nightmarish atmosphere; this, for our cowardly private, is the beginning of a journey of expiation. He meets a "tattered soldier" whose wounds and embarrassing questions increase his sense of guilt. The two men are caught up in the procession of wounded soldiers who make their way to the rear. Among them they see Henry's friend, Jim Conklin, the mortally wounded "tall soldier" who, after horrible sufferings climaxed by a gruesome "danse macabre," dies under their petrified gaze. After this shattering experience Henry abandons the "tattered man" whose very presence seems to him an accusation. Retreating Union soldiers fly past him and one of them, whom the youth tries to question, knocks him down with the butt of his rifle, ironically giving him the "red badge of courage" he had been longing for. After regaining consciousness Henry meets a man with "a cheery voice" who takes him back to his regiment and, from then on, the protagonist's attitude is altogether changed. He feels full of aggressive but specious self-confidence and, because he does not reveal the real cause of his wound, derives much unmerited respect from his fellow soldiers for his ostensibly courageous conduct. The last chapters show him turning into a daredevil, fighting at the head of his unit during a victorious charge, but at the end of the story – which is no pamphlet for recruiting officers – Henry's regiment finds itself recrossing the river it had crossed a few days before and thus going back to its previous position on the other bank of the Rappahannock as if nothing had happened. Henry's first impression had been right after all: "It was all a trap."

A constant ironic counterpoint aims to debunk the traditional concept of glorious war. The whole thing seems absurd: generals shout, stammer, and behave childishly on the battlefield; Henry's wound confers upon him a spurious glory; Wilson, the "loud soldier," has become as meek as a lamb in the last chapters, and the whole tumult has resulted in no gain of ground for the Union forces and no loss for the Confederates. What remains in the mind of the reader is a series of confused movements with, from time to time, "men drop[ping] here and there like bundles" and, in the protagonist's "procession of memory," sad nerve-racking images suddenly blurred with a sense of relief when the "sultry nightmare [is] in the past."

Like all the great classics of literature *The Red Badge of Courage* speaks of different things to different minds. However, only an oversimplified interpretation could see in Henry's final charge the proof that he has become, as he himself thinks, "a man." The pattern of this book is that of a spiritual journey, but the final goal remains in doubt when we reach the conclusion: "Over the river a golden ray of sun came through the hosts of leaden rain clouds." The youth, in his baptism of fire, has acquired self-knowledge and experience, but a radical change has not taken place within him: he remains, in his heroic pose at the end, just as grotesque as the fearful "little man" he was at the beginning. The dialogue he has been carrying on with his own conscience often contains overtones of legalistic chicanery: it is a constant search for excuses to justify his cowardly conduct. Occasional flashes of inner sincerity are defeated by his attempts to demonstrate that what he did was logically and morally valid, but his arguments would fail to convince anyone and only add to his torment. Through a series of excruciating experiences which follow his shameful act he manages to keep his secret and even to rise in stature in the eyes of his regiment. But, instead of closing the book with a reassuring epiphany, the author preserves the ironic structure throughout. Henry's conscience is still disturbed when the book ends, and his concealed guilt spoils "the gilded images of memory."

The Red Badge of Courage contains the account of a half-completed conversion. It is only in a satellite story entitled "The Veteran" that Henry pays the full price for his "sin" and goes through the final stage of his itinerary of redemption. Then, by belatedly but unequivocally confessing his lack of courage on the battlefield, he purges himself of his former lie. In the last scene of "The Veteran," determined to save two colts trapped in his burning barn, he plunges into the flames never to come out, thus making a gesture of genuine and unconventional bravery. Rejecting his previous irony, Crane presents here a real conversion, grounded on cool, selfless determination and not on spurious enthusiasm as was Henry's sudden reversal of mood on the battlefield.

In Crane's war novel religious imagery prevails, centered on an itinerary of spiritual redemption which leads not to eternal salvation but to a blissful impasse. Alone in the middle of the forest the hero discovers the imaginary "chapel" with its "columnlike" trees where a "hymn of twilight" is heard. When the "tall soldier" dies, wildly gesturing in his final agony, he seems to resemble "a devotee of a mad religion"; most significant in the same creative process is Henry's illusion after his cowardly flight: he looks for "a means of escape from the consequences of his fall" and, unable to reach redemption through mere introspection, returns to "the creed of soldiers." But his final charge does not purge him of his guilt in spite of a temporary exultation due to the repression of his fear; "the ghost of his flight" and "a specter of reproach" born of the desertion of "the tattered man" in his sorest need keep haunting the youth at the close of the book. Some obvious similarities with the theme of concealment in Hawthorne's fiction can also be noted: "veil" metaphors and similes clustered around the character of Henry Fleming keep recurring in the narrative. In Chapter I the hero "wish[es] to be alone with some new thoughts that [have] lately come to him"; in Chapter VII he "cring[es] as if discovered in a crime" and, under the burden of his hidden guilt, soon feels that "his shame [can] be viewed." But an ironic glimmer of hope reappears in his consciousness when he imagines that "in the battle blur" his face will be hidden "like the face of a cowled man."

Beside this procession of religious images there appears here and there a scattering of scenes with animal characters which seem to be fables in miniature. The style abounds in symbolic rabbits, squirrels, horses, cows, and snakes which form a conventional bestiary by the side of a Christian demonology swarming with monsters directly borrowed from Biblical literature.

Another facet of this book is its consistent use of legalistic terminology. A dossier is being minutely, if inconclusively, revealed to us: the youth of this story approaches his problem of fear in a logical manner and determines to "accumulate information of himself"; at first he tries to "mathematically prove to himself that he [will] not run from a battle." Then, after experiencing his shameful flight, he acts as his own lawyer and attempts to present a convincing defense of his case: "He had done a good part in saving himself, who was a little part of the army. . . . His actions had been sagacious things. They had been full of strategy. They were the work of a master's legs." A strong ironic coloring, one of the main characteristics of Crane's style in the whole book, can easily be detected here. Henry is constantly trying to show his actions to advantage; when he returns to his regiment after his cowardly escape, he even considers using the "small weapon" — a packet of letters — which Wilson in a panic had left in his hands before the battle. This "exhibit" would, Henry thinks, "prostrate his comrade at the first signs of a cross-examination."

The mechanistic imagery of *The Red Badge of Courage* already adumbrates the development of Crane's war motif in his writings after the Cuban conflict of 1898, and serves to highlight the complexity and destructiveness of modern war: "The battle was like the grinding of an immense and terrible machine to him. Its complexities and powers, its grim processes, fascinated him. He must go close and see it produce corpses."

If military courage had been one of the values pitilessly probed in *The Red Badge of Courage,* it also furnished the central topic for a satellite story entitled "A Mystery of Heroism." Private Fred Collins ventures into no man's land under the pretext of procuring some water for his company; but in fact his action has been prompted by the desire to prove to himself that he is not "afraid t' go." After being "blindly . . . led by quaint emotions" he returns unscathed to his lines, but the author wastes no sympathy on his "heroic" deed. "Death and the Child" deals with the same theme, the scene being now the Greco-Turkish war of 1897; the central character, a war correspondent, soon sees his battle fury die out and, instead of fighting by the side of the soldiers of his mother country, flees and encounters a child who asks him this embarrassing question: "Are you a man?"

In his reporting of the same war and of the Cuban conflict Crane fell in with the conventions of his time and did not aim at more than ordinary journalistic style. But when reworking his factual accounts of battles and recollecting his war experiences in tranquillity he achieved the spare and severe economy of *Wounds in the Rain,* a moving and realistic adaptation in fiction of his own adventures with the American forces sent to Cuba in 1898. His protagonist then ceased to be a dreamy amateur like Henry Fleming in *The Red Badge* or Peza in "Death and the Child," and the figure of Private Nolan, the regular, as anonymous and unromantic as any true regular, stood out in the foreground. Crane was now dealing with war as a special trade, and his soldiers at work were shown to be "as deliberate and exact as so many watchmakers." In "The Price of the Harness" he went beyond the phantasmagoria of his early definition of war and made of "a great, grand steel loom . . . to weave a woof of thin red threads, the cloth of death," the essential metaphor of his battle symbolics. Henceforth, in the logbook of the war correspondent, what had been in *The Red Badge* a "monster," a "dragon," or a "blood-swollen god," gradually came down to the lowly estate of "death, and a plague of the lack of small things and toil." Crane could not have gone any further in deglamorizing that image of "vague and bloody conflicts" which had once "thrilled [Henry Fleming] with their sweep and fire."

A gradual reduction of the concept of war to the archetype can be found in Crane's later stories, if we leave aside as mere potboiling and unoriginal work his *Great Battles of the World.* It is in the "Spitzbergen Tales" that the war metaphor is suddenly brought down to its essentials, the taking of a coveted hill, the storming of a redoubt, or a burial scene on the front line. The typical hero of most of these stories is no longer a private but a noncommissioned or low-ranking officer, the problem of conduct being then studied in an almost abstract context and the main issue being the duty of the responsible professional toward his command. Primarily concerned with war as a personal test, Crane avoided the approach of the historian, that of the strategist, and deliberately worked out that of the moralist.

To him war, in its various manifestations, was the alpha and omega of human life, essentially a testing ground, but adventure could be a fair substitute. Sent to the West and Mexico by the Bacheller Syndicate as a roving reporter early in 1895, he drew upon his tour for a few outstanding stories. His shipwreck off the coast of Florida in January 1897 furnished material for "The Open Boat," a tale which won immediate recognition and found in Conrad and H. G. Wells two faithful admirers. The latter even went so far as to say about it: "[It is], to my mind, beyond all question, the crown of all his work."

Stephen Crane depended on adventure, vicarious or real, as fodder for his imagination. He had to *feel* intensely to *write* intensely. As soon as the pace of his life became relaxed because of illness and a general weakening of his spiritual energy, he was compelled to turn to his childhood reminiscences, also fraught with intense emotions, or to an archetypal war metaphor in order to write successfully.

The short stories "The Blue Hotel," "The Bride Comes to Yellow Sky," and "The Open Boat" outline his personal attitude toward the literary utilization of experience. Although fond of exotic settings and people Crane is not a local colorist. The colors of his adventures are the colors of his soul. For example the real fight that he saw in a saloon in Lincoln, Nebraska, which is supposed to have been the germ of "The Blue Hotel," was transmuted by him into a moral study on the theme of collective and individual responsibility. The narrative in this tale is conducted on two levels, straight storytelling and ironic counterpoint. A Swede who has lived for ten years in New York and is now traveling in the West experiences forebodings of violent death and is eventually justified in his fear, since he meets his doom at the hands of a professional gambler. Crane, however, succeeds in keeping up the suspense by leading his main character into ominous situations at the Palace Hotel which are ironically deflated and prove harmless to the frightened hero. Once the latter feels that all danger is over and is about to celebrate his escape from the hotel in a neighboring saloon, he is stabbed to death by a gambler whom he wanted too insistently to befriend. Crane here comes back once again to an analysis of fear. In the Swede's mind this feeling follows a pattern similar to that of Henry's itinerary in *The Red Badge*: from timidity to unrestrained arrogance. Both Henry and the Swede are intoxicated, the former with a belatedly discovered battle fury, the latter with repeated drinking. Crane also explores the comic overtones of violence, and notes the grotesque fall of the Swede's body, "pierced as easily as if it had been a melon." The protagonist obviously brought about his own destruction, but the writer is not just censuring one man's attitude, and the easterner, Mr. Blanc, who acts as point-of-view character, declares: " 'We are all in it! . . . Every sin is the result of a collaboration.' " Once again the creator of *Maggie* stigmatized the unpardonable sin, indifference: no one had done anything to prevent the final denouement from taking place. The hotelkeeper and the bartender had provided drink; the other "collaborators," Johnnie excepted, since he had been most active in arousing the Swede's anger, had each exhibited a different form of passivity.

"One Dash — Horses" is another study of fear, this time in a Mexican setting. In its gaudy and alluring garb this tale reads like a direct transcript of experience, but the narrative is not limited to the account of a thrilling manhunt; Crane is more interested in exploring the psychological springs of fear and the power of illusion. The young American and his guide are afraid of the Mexican bandits, and the latter are terrorized by the thought of the mounted police — the "rurales" — but it is an abstract stereotype of the traditional enemy which causes this feeling in both cases. The Mexican bandits prove to be playthings in the hands of the gods, and the arrival of a group of prostitutes scatters to the winds their plans of murder and plunder; later on, when their lust has been appeased and they have resumed the chase, a detachment of rurales frightens them away without firing a single shot. The real power of the story lies in its subtle use of irony and in its cascading evocations of fear in a Western-style pursuit.

In "The Bride Comes to Yellow Sky" Crane reached a peak in his exploration of the humorous overtones of fear. A favorite of the author himself and of many of his admirers, "The Bride" raises the western story to the level of the classic by consistently applying to a trite but dramatic situation the powerful lever of irony. It deals with a very unromantic event, the homecoming of a town marshal after his wedding with a plain-looking and timid bride. This town marshal is afraid of nothing except public opinion and, since his marriage was secretly arranged, he fears the hostile reaction of the inhabitants of Yellow Sky, an obvious projection of Crane's own predicament in his life with Cora. When, after walking through the deserted town, the couple reach the door of their home, they meet Scratchy Wilson, the local outlaw. A bloody encounter to come, we might think, but in fact nothing happens: the outlaw is defeated by the mere sight of the town marshal seen for the first time as a married man and walking home unarmed. "Defeated by a woman's mute presence" might have been the headline for such a story if it had been printed in a "yellow" newspaper. Crane thought that "The Bride" was "a daisy," and he was right. From beginning to end this charming tale proves that the whole mystique of the wild West was for him nothing but a game, and he enjoyed watching this game in its closing stages.

But no judgment of Crane's ability as a storyteller can be reached without a proper assessment of "a tale intended to be after the fact" entitled "The Open Boat," which relates the concluding phase of an almost fatal adventure. The newspaper report he sent to the *New York Press* in January 1897, immediately after his shipwreck, gave a detailed account of every episode excluding the "thirty hours" spent in an open boat. It took a few weeks for the definitive story to crystallize in his mind as a parable of human existence. We follow the ordeal of four survivors during their long wait in a lifeboat, their desperate attempts to reach the shore after their ship has sunk. Finally the captain decides to risk steering the frail dinghy through the breakers: the four men — the captain, the cook, the oiler, and the correspondent — have, each of them, felt the "subtle brotherhood" born of their shared distress and struggle. Once in the breakers the boat is overturned and the oiler is killed. The other three set foot safely ashore. Crane never wrote a more orderly tale: the correspondent, acting as point-of-view character — although he is also a participant — helps to bring the main facets of the story into focus. We learn much about the transformation of his mind in the crucible of experience. This shipwreck is for him a journey leading from cynicism to humility. But here again Crane retains the ironic approach, especially when he shows the correspondent's indignation leveled at the serene indifference of God. "Shipwrecks are *apropos* of nothing" puts into a nutshell the meaning of the whole story. There is the world of facts on one side and the world of ideas and literature on the other, but facts as such do not exist to *prove* anything. However, some lessons can be drawn from the chaos of experience if men manage to be "interpreters." Crane's message here is one of endurance, brotherhood, and stoic acceptance of man's fate; his vision of the universe is one in which man appears frail and insignificant when isolated but surprisingly strong in a united effort. Ruthlessly debunking all the conventional views about heroism, he seems to imply that the only courage worthy of esteem is unobtrusive, silent, and more self-denying than self-assertive.

The true power of this story comes from a style which, in descriptive passages, is almost that of a prose poem. The dialogue, spare and accurate, gives balance to the general tone. According to Edward Garnett, Crane's art at its best was "self-poising as is the art of the perfect dancer." Joined to the grace of the dancer we find in this tale of human frailty a superb control of emotion which makes it a masterpiece of classical art, the epic flow of the narrative being constantly tempered and toned down by gentle touches of irony.

There always remained in Crane, as Alfred Kazin has pointed out, "a local village boy." Essentially American in his stance, although a rebel against many things American, he willingly spoke about his experience of the small town. Far from idealizing his vision, he set it against the background of his urban and cosmopolitan environment and judged it unemotionally.

The Crane brothers loved the countryside of Sullivan County, New York, where they fished, hunted, rode horses, and camped during the summer months. The hills, mountains, and valleys of this still rather wild area form a recurrent image in many of Stephen Crane's stories, poems, and prose poems. Although he used this background indirectly in his fiction, he made of it the infrastructure of his vision of the world.

The Third Violet reflects a deep attachment to the colors and shapes of Sullivan County. It exploits both the popular theme of the "summer hotel" and Crane's own experience at the Art Students' League in New York. In this novel the author has captured some of the flavor of bohemianism, but his treatment of this subject lacks originality. *The Third Violet,* which won very little applause from critics except for Ford Madox Hueffer, is saved from mediocrity by contrasting vignettes of rural and urban life. This book hints at the difficult struggle of young artists with the commercial values of their age: Hawker, a young painter, goes to Sullivan County where his farmer parents live; he is merely in search of peace and inspiration but, in a neighboring hotel, the summer has brought adventure in the shape of a rich New York heiress, Miss Fanhall. It is love at first sight and the novel abounds in meetings and vapid conversations between the two lovers and a few other characters, a "writing friend" of Hawker's called Hollanden, a rival in love, named Oglethorpe, who is the irresistible rich suitor, and a group of irresponsible young artists belonging to Hawker's circle in New York. Among the latter stands out a rather colorful young model in love with Hawker, Florinda. We close the book unconvinced by the plot which, with the gift of a final violet symbolizing the reconciliation of the two lovers, seems to be heading for a conventional epilogue. Crane did not want his novel to end tragically as his real-life romance with Nellie Crouse had done.

"The Monster," a story set in a rural background, can be regarded as one of the most important of his short works. It is centered on the disastrous consequences of a generous action: a doctor's son has been rescued from his burning house by a Negro servant, Henry Johnson, whose face is "burned away." Out of gratitude the doctor decides to nurse his heroic servant and insists on keeping him in his reconstructed house, but the sight of the "monster" frightens everyone in the neighborhood; the doctor soon becomes an object of opprobrium and loses much of his practice. A deputation of influential citizens tries to persuade him to compromise with public opinion and asks him to turn Henry over to an institution, but the doctor remains adamant. The last scene shows him returning from his rounds and finding his wife crying over the teacups of guests who have not come. This brilliant exposition of village mores is enhanced by symbolic touches which, in the laboratory scene during the fire, reach a climax with the lurid vision of threatening and fantastically colored shapes. Besides the fear born of physical danger, the author probes the blind unreasoning panic generated by the sight of the harmless and horribly maimed Negro, and the many anxieties caused by public opinion. He has also, by the very choice of his protagonist, indicated that true heroism is not the privilege of the whites alone.

Crane began reminiscing about his early youth when he had used up the store of material born of his adult experience. Port Jervis, New York, was the nucleus around which *The Whilomville Stories* took shape. It is "any boy's town" but also a very specific one within easy reach of New York City, yet quite provincial and sleepy with its backdrop of fields, rivers, hills, and forests, a place where boys and girls can roam at peace except when under the ferule of their school or Sunday school teachers. The fields are close by and the farmers' slow and benevolent manner offers a sharp contrast with the "barbarous" habits of the villagers who give tea parties, launch into charitable campaigns, and, in the summertime, entertain relatives from the city.

The rural life depicted by Crane is more civilized than that Mark Twain had evoked before him; it is less sentimentally reconstructed than the *Boy's Town* of W. D. Howells. Abhorring as he did the "Little Lord Fauntleroy" craze which had swept his country in the 1880's, Crane did not hesitate to show us real children. He is aware of their tastes and distastes and conscious of their cruelty—at times they appear to him as "little blood-fanged wolves." In fact, more than a picture of childhood, he gives a picture of town life, since the children project an image of their parents' world stripped to its essentials. Although fond of the company of youngsters and a great favorite with his nieces, Crane was not holding a brief in favor of youth. To quote Robert Frost out of context he "lov[ed] the things he love[d] for what they [were]"; his children were, like their adult counterparts, charmingly deluded in their vision of the world, and we can safely smile at their innocent pranks, for Crane did not allow them to give free rein to their worst instincts. At the critical moment something happened: a bully relented or an adult came into view, and none of these little dramas of the backyard turned into a real tragedy.

By profession a journalist and a writer of fiction, Crane had a higher regard for his poetic endeavors than for the rest of his literary work. He preferred his first volume of verse, *The Black Riders,* to his *Red Badge of Courage* because "it was a more ambitious effort. My aim was to comprehend in it the thoughts I have had about life in general while 'The Red Badge' is a mere episode in life, an amplification."

But he did not observe the traditions and conventions of poetic expression respected by most of his contemporaries, except isolated rebels like Walt Whitman and Emily Dickinson. Alfred Kazin has called Crane "our first *poète maudit*" and such a label fits him to perfection, for he regarded poetry, more than prose, as a vehicle for ideas generally unconventional or iconoclastic.

It is easy to find models for the patterns if not for the tone of Crane's early verse. He had obviously read Biblical parables, and some of the work of Emily Dickinson, Whitman, Ambrose Bierce, and Olive Schreiner, but his poetry remained essentially the expression of his own vision.

The sharpness and brevity of the sixty-eight pieces forming his *Black Riders* remind many readers of Emily Dickinson's great verbal economy. Like that of the poetess of Amherst his voice was one of protest. His own rebellion went against the God of the Old Testament, and he strove to debunk a cluster of false values, especially ambition, conformity, worldly wisdom, military glory, and traditional religion. The universe pictured by Crane in his poetry has elements of pessimism which have caused some critics to regard it as naturalistic, but the poet also exalts the positive virtues of love, endurance, and self-reliance. Crane feels a great admiration for the "little man" who keeps facing the mountains fearlessly, for the lonely individualist who "sought a new road" and "died thus alone," for "they said he had courage." The first themes of his poetic vision radiate from a central concern, the problem of man's relation with God. Even earthly love can be poisoned by the idea of sin and man must free himself from his obsessive fear of God and from the network of illusions woven by his imagination. Crane's rebellion was sound but the occasionally crude phrasing of his protest and the printing of the volume in small capitals made it fair game for the parodists.

His second book of poetry, *War Is Kind,* contained thirty-seven poems: fourteen of these had already been printed between 1895 and 1898; a group of ten love poems called "Intrigue" and some of the remaining pieces belonged to a second poetic output. The iconoclastic note had not died out and the author went on debunking the outward forms of religious ritual:

> You tell me this is God?
> I tell you this is a printed list,
> A burning candle and an ass.

But his poetry gradually became more concrete and more socially oriented. Instead of dealing with abstract imaginings, vague and remote parables, it drank deep from the fountain of experience. His bitter satire on the popular glorification of military courage in such a poem as "War Is Kind" (which, although the initial piece in the second volume, belongs to the first period) had been expressed along general lines. With the "The Blue Battalions" and the poems inspired by the Spanish-American war, Crane did not hesitate to present war as the utmost form of God's playful fancy and violently denounced the exploitation of "patriots" by "practical men" as well as the imperialistic overtones of America's help to the Cuban rebels.

Several poems stigmatized other forms of exploitation of man by man. The gaudy and showy splendor of the mansions of the new rich aroused his metaphoric ire with a vision of

> . . . a crash of flunkeys
> And yawning emblems of Persia
> Cheeked against oak, France and a sabre,
> The outcry of old beauty
> Whored by pimping merchants
> To submission before wine and chatter.

And he ironically rejected the basic injustice of laissez-faire economics:

> Why should the strong –
> – The beautiful strong –
> Why should they not have the flowers?

If the theme of love had, in the poems of the first poetic manner, taken on few romantic dimensions except in the sheltering gesture of a woman's "white arms," the second volume of verse and some posthumous poems enable us to probe deeper into Crane's house of love. "On the desert" and "A naked woman and a dead dwarf" fly the banner of Baudelairean decadence most clearly and remind us of "La femme et le serpent" and, as has been recently pointed out, of a prose poem by the French symbolist entitled "Le fou et la Vénus." "Intrigue," the last section of *War Is Kind*, represents Crane's attempt to bring into focus the many components of his love poetry: sensuality, sin-consciousness, and jealousy form the dark side of man's central passion, but Crane's bitter lyricism is spoiled by hackneyed romantic imagery, skulls "with ruby eyes," cracked bowls, castles, temples, daggers, and specters.

He discovered a better instrument for his highly sensitive nature in the prose poem. "The Judgment of the Sage" and "The Snake" are true fables and the same ingredients are found in them as in his verse; but, whereas the verse rejects all traditional rules (rhyme, regular meter, and very often stanzaic form), the prose poems retain a classical mode of expression. They remind us of Baudelaire's utilization of the same medium, but here again Crane's manner remains distinctly his own. He thus studied some archetypes, those of charity, material success, earthly conflict or cosmic battle. "The Judgment of the Sage," which raises the ghost of a Kantian dilemma, briefly tells us the story of a vain quest, that of worldly wisdom. Should we practice charity "because of God's word" or because the beggar is hungry? Crane does not solve this riddle; God seems to play with man his eternal game of hide-and-seek and keeps him on the run. "A Self-Made Man" parodies the Horatio Alger type of success story. " 'To succeed in life . . . the youth of America have only to see an old man seated upon a railing and smoking a clay pipe. Then go up and ask him for a match.' " "The Voice of the Mountain" and "The Victory of the Moon" are focused on the conflict between man and a mysterious cosmic power which can occasionally be defeated by "the little creature of the earth." With "The Snake" the inevitable fight for survival is brought to its emotional climax: the two most antagonistic creatures in the world, man and the snake, confront each other in a ruthless duel in which the principals fight with equal arms, the snake with its venom and man with his stick. If the snake is defeated it is not for lack of courage. Thanks to a clever manipulation of language Crane combines in a unified whole the simplicity of the fable, the logical structure of the sermon, and the raciness of the tall tale.

His poetry at times foreshadows Imagism, as Carl Sandburg pointed out in his "Letters to Dead Imagists," but some pieces of the second volume of verse show a tendency to explode the small abstract capsule of the early poems. It is difficult to say where Crane's real poetic genius lies, whether in his spare, concise parables, in his longer symbolistic compositions, or in his prose poems. He worshiped brevity as the first tenet of his literary creed, but he was also touched by the wave of decadent aesthetics that Copeland and Day, his publishers, who were also the American publishers of the *Yellow Book,* had helped to introduce into the United States. There was, however, too much love of moral integrity in Crane for him to become a true decadent. In his verse he often displayed the pathetic agony of a fallen albatross, but the prose poem was perhaps the literary instrument whose scope and subtle rhythm best suited his genius.

Crane's style has a certain number of idiosyncrasies: it is primarily the language of a writer in transition betraying an inner conflict between a romantic tradition and realistic impulses. He began with what he called his "Rudyard-Kipling style" and the "Sullivan County Sketches" contain the germs of most of his future work, displaying as they do a love of abstraction and a systematic use of color, patterning the narrative with structural irony, and building up an oneiric atmosphere laden with threat. It is a gradual mastery of form that we witness in the passage from the style of the early years to that emerging between 1894 and 1898.

Impelled by a desire to control the deep stirrings of his soul, he soon declared that he wished "to write plainly and unmistakably, so that all men (and some women) might read and understand." Crane's literary aesthetics was close to that of the French master of the short story, Guy de Maupassant. According to the author of *Pierre et Jean*, "Les grands artistes sont ceux qui imposent à l'humanité leur illusion particulière." Such a position might very well have been defined by Stephen Crane who wanted the writer to tell the world what "his own pair of eyes" enabled him to see and nothing else. Maupassant's universe, however, differed significantly from Crane's: whereas the French writer often indulged in an excess of sensual evocations, Crane preserved throughout his writing career the viewpoint of the moralist and usually conveyed his ethical comments by means of ironic counterpoint.

He was deeply conscious of man's littleness and of God's overbearing power. Man's wanderings on the earth were pictured by him as those of a lonely pilgrim in a pathless universe. Crane's phraseology comes directly from the Bible, the sermons, and the hymns which had shaped his language during his youth. The topography of his stories, where hills, mountains, rivers, and meadows appear under symbolic suns or moons is, to a large extent, an abstraction fraught with religious or moral significance. With its "monsters" of various kinds and its "dragons," the demonology of *The Red Badge of Courage* evinces a truly apocalyptic quality. In Crane's best work the imagery of the journey of initiation occupies a central position and reaches a climactic stage with some experience of conversion. He did not accept, it is true, the traditional interpretation of the riddle of the universe offered by the Methodist church. Nevertheless he constantly used a Christian terminology, and the thought of "sin" inspired his characters with guilty fears and stirred up within them such frequent debates with a troubled conscience that it is impossible to study his achievement outside a religious tradition.

But he did not remain a prisoner of the stylistic patterns which he derived from his revivalist heritage. New York street life very early made an impact on his language, which thus acquired its liveliness and its ability to picture violence in colorful terms. Crane's dialogues abound in expletives, in stereotyped phrases, in phonetic transcriptions of common verbal corruptions and dialectal idiosyncrasies. Yet they never fall into the trap of over-specialization. His ear was good, whether he listened to Irish, German, Italian, or Cuban immigrants in New York, to farmers in Sullivan County, or to Negroes in Port Jervis, but he never tried to achieve a perfect rendering of local dialect. In *The Red Badge of Courage* he used dialogue to introduce some degree of differentiation between Henry Fleming and his comrades but, on the whole, Crane's characters all speak one language which is Crane's own, a youthful and casual version of the American vernacular of the 1890's often heard in artists' studios and among students.

Language is in the mouths of his central characters a stylized medium carrying universal overtones, and this trait reveals an essential aspect of his fictional techniques, namely the dramatic approach. He tried his hand several times at playwriting and, although his various attempts in this literary genre were of modest stature, he was naturally inclined to work out his tales and some of his verse in terms of stage stylistics. He completed three very slight plays. *At Clancy's Wake* (1893) is a one-act sketch which brings to life the hilarious moments of an Irish wake in New York; *The Blood of the Martyr* (1898) satirizes in three brief acts German imperialistic policies in China. Another attempt at playwriting was his "Spanish-American War Play," unpublished in Crane's lifetime but recently included in *The War Dispatches of Stephen Crane* (1964): this two-act drama gives a mildly amusing but superficial picture of stereotyped national traits against the background of a real conflict that the author had seen at first hand. Only a fragment of the text of "The Ghost" – his English play – has reached us so far and it is difficult to take seriously what was meant to be a mere Christmas entertainment. All his other attempts at playwriting were abortive.

What remains most striking in Crane's style considered as a whole is a concern for brevity and a constant use of irony which serves a twofold purpose: it provides his best work with tightly knit thematic structures and reveals his tacit belief in a rigid set of values which condemns indifference and conformism, and extols moral courage and integrity.

Seen in the perspective of the years which have elapsed since his death, Crane's work is surprisingly modern. His influence on the war literature of the twentieth century in England and America has been very significant. Many of Hemingway's novels and short stories disclose a similar preoccupation with "the moral problem of conduct" and obvious stylistic affinities; distinct echoes of *The Red Badge* can be heard in *A Farewell to Arms.* In England we could trace recurring correspondences in the work of Joseph Conrad and Ford Madox Ford. Ford, like Conrad, had been a good friend of Crane's during the last three years of his life, and both defended his literary and moral reputation in magazine articles or prefaces after his death. The plight of the isolated hero, which became a favorite theme of Conrad's, stemmed directly from *The Red Badge of Courage.* Obsession with the fear of showing a white feather haunted the soul of the author of *Lord Jim* as much as that of the creator of Henry Fleming. In his own fiction Ford Madox Ford used complex techniques and mixed many strands of life, but some of the most dramatic scenes in *A Man Could Stand Up,* which are mere vignettes of life at the front, remind us in their bare and rugged prose of deliberately unpoetic descriptions of war in *The Red Badge.* Like Crane, Ford emphasized "the eternal waiting that is War" and the crippling effects of noise on a battlefield. And, in order to describe the subtle change taking place in a soldier's mind, he used almost Cranean terms.

Among the pioneers of the "free-verse army" Crane is often neglected by anthologists or literary critics. Yet he gave to the poetry of his country the patterns and rhythms of an "exasperated prose" that foreshadows modern poetic expression.

Carl Van Doren wrote in 1924: "Modern American literature may be said, accurately enough, to have begun with Stephen Crane." This statement needs to be qualified, but Crane was one of the leading figures of protest of his generation and thus showed the way to American liberalism. His influence in the field of the novel has affected a mode of thought rather than literary techniques, if we leave aside his synaesthetic use of imagery which survives almost intact in F. Scott Fitzgerald. Crane's impact has been felt mostly in the genre of the short story, for which he displayed a personal preference. "The Blue Hotel," "The Bride Comes to Yellow Sky," and, above all, "The Open Boat" are some of the finest models of American literary achievement in this genre, and the greatest successes of Faulkner, Sherwood Anderson, Hemingway, Fitzgerald, and other modern

American short story writers hark back to these models. Accuracy in details, conciseness, and effective rendering, framed and supported by an ironic structure, are now frequently regarded as essential requirements by American practitioners of the short story.

Most of Crane's work could be explained in terms of his religious background and he always betrays, even in his most sportive mood, the serious preoccupations of the born moralist. However, his slum stories, instead of aiming to move the reader by exaggerated pathos and convert him to the cause of reform, wish to convert him to the cause of psychological truth; social implications are left for the reader to discover but are not explicitly stated. When dealing with his main theme, war, he gradually worked out a revolutionary stand, doing away with externals and reducing human conflict to a classic drama of internal forces struggling with elemental powers. From Henry Fleming in *The Red Badge* to Timothy Lean in the "Spitzbergen Tales" the itinerary of heroism evolves from a path sprinkled with doubtful victories to a road doggedly followed with a sturdy and silent acceptance of personal responsibility; diseased and action-hampering introspection eventually gives way to selfless and unassuming patterns of affirmation. "The Open Boat" contains a plea for human solidarity and *Wounds in the Rain*, in spite of a persistent and depressing background of military servitude, discreetly affirms the superiority of collective to individual prowess. A subtle feeling of warmth and brotherhood pervades the later studies of Crane on war; even "The Upturned Face," a macabre piece which describes a burial scene on the front line, places the reader in the midst of an ultimate manifestation of soldierly brotherhood.

It is in the novel of manners that Crane's achievement is at its lowest ebb. He did not try to study complex human relationships born of urban settings but dealt with a few basic themes, rivalries between lovers, or conflicts between generations and social classes. Often unable to provide his puppets with life, he proved his mastery in the art of reproducing informal dialogue. He experimented in the field of the picaresque novel – a medium he had already used in several short stories – but *The O'Ruddy* cannot be regarded as a genuine offspring of his mind since Robert Barr gave this novel its conclusion and ultimate form.

Crane's identity runs no risk of being drowned in a backflow of imitators, because his style remains his own. His unerring eye for color, his brilliant use of synaesthetic effects, his love for the potent metaphor made him controversially famous in his lifetime and now stamp him as a truly original artist. His sometimes erratic grammar no longer shocks us, while his cinematic techniques have come into their own.

It was his aim to underline elements of absurdity in human life, and his work contains disquieting overtones for sedate minds. His was a voice of dissent which rejected the ostensibly impregnable soundness of historical Christianity, the conventional vision of a well-ordered society and that genteel tradition of culture which never left drawing rooms and libraries. Crane inherited the New England habit of individual assertion. He fits well into the American liberal tradition and can, in some respects, be regarded as a spiritual son of Emerson. Any form of dogmatism in any field of human life seemed to him both childish and harmful to what he valued above everything else, the integrity of the human soul. No problem could, according to him, ever find a definitive solution and he had certainly listened to Emerson's advice: "Congratulate yourself if you have done something strange and extravagant, and broken the monotony of a decorous age." This sentence adorned a beam in one of the studios of the old Art Students' League building in New York where

Crane lived sporadically in 1893 and 1894. Above and beyond this cult of nonconformism is another idea of Emerson's which involves the deeper regions of the soul: "Always do what you are afraid to do." Crane put this motto into practice so consistently that he wrecked his health and seriously endangered his moral reputation in his own country.

His recent popularity, essentially due to a revival of critical interest during the 1950's, should help prepare the ground for a clearer assessment of Crane's achievement. To our generation he can still teach moral integrity, a revised conception of courage, and psychological truth, all the more effectively because he did not resort to traditional didactic devices. He can also show modern prose writers the flexibility of the English language and encourage them to make linguistic experiments and create a language free from any excessive tyranny of the past, perfectly in tune with the spirit of the age and yet retaining the robust vitality which is the trademark of the classic.

Selected Bibliography

Works of Stephen Crane

NOVELS

Maggie: A Girl of the Streets (A Story of New York) by Johnston Smith (pseud.). N.p. [1893]. Revised ed., *Maggie: A Girl of the Streets.* New York: Appleton, 1896. There have been three recent reprints of note: one edited by Joseph Katz (Gainesville, Fla.: Scholars' Facsimiles and Reprints, 1966); another by Maurice Bassan (*Stephen Crane's Maggie, Text and Context,* Belmont, Calif.: Wadsworth Publication, 1966); and the latest by Donald Pizer (San Francisco: Chandler, 1968).

The Red Badge of Courage. New York: Appleton, 1895.

George's Mother. New York and London: Edward Arnold, 1896.

The Third Violet. New York: Appleton, 1897.

Active Service. New York: Frederick A. Stokes, 1899.

The O'Ruddy. New York: Frederick A. Stokes, 1903.

The Complete Novels of Stephen Crane, edited by Thomas A. Gullason. New York: Doubleday, 1967.

SHORT STORIES AND SKETCHES

The Little Regiment and Other Episodes of the American Civil War. New York: Appleton, 1896.

The Open Boat and Other Tales of Adventure. New York: Doubleday and McClure, 1898.

The Monster and Other Stories. New York: Harper, 1899. (Contains only "The Monster," "The Blue Hotel," and "His New Mittens.")

Whilomville Stories. New York and London: Harper, 1900.

Wounds in the Rain. New York: Frederick A. Stokes, 1900.

Great Battles of the World. Philadelphia: Lippincott, 1901.

The Monster. London: Harper, 1901. (Contains "The Monster," "The Blue Hotel," "His New Mittens," "Twelve O'Clock," "Moonlight on the Snow," "Manacled," and "An Illusion in Red and White.")

Last Words. London: Digby, Long, 1902.

Men, Women and Boats, edited with an introduction by Vincent Starrett. New York: Boni and Liveright, 1917. (Contains seventeen stories and sketches.)

A Battle in Greece. Mount Vernon, N.Y.: Peter Pauper Press, 1936. (Contains a reprint of the battle sketch which appeared in the *New York Journal* of June 13, 1897.)

The Sullivan County Sketches, edited by Melvin Schoberlin. Syracuse, N.Y.: Syracuse University Press, 1949.

The Complete Short Stories and Sketches of Stephen Crane, edited by Thomas A. Gullason. New York: Doubleday, 1963.

The New York City Sketches of Stephen Crane and Related Pieces, edited by R. W. Stallman and E. R. Hagemann. New York: New York University Press, 1966.

Stephen Crane: Sullivan County Tales and Sketches, edited by R. W. Stallman. Ames: Iowa State University Press, 1968.

WAR DISPATCHES

The War Dispatches of Stephen Crane, edited by R. W. Stallman and E. R. Hagemann. New York: New York University Press, 1964.

POETRY AND PLAYS

The Black Riders and Other Lines. Boston: Copeland and Day, 1895.

A Souvenir and a Medley. East Aurora, N.Y.: Roycroft Printing Shop, 1896. (Contains seven poems, as well as a sketch entitled "A Great Mistake" and a fifteen-line piece printed in capitals, "A Prologue," which reads like stage directions.)

War Is Kind. New York: Frederick A. Stokes, 1899.

The Collected Poems of Stephen Crane, edited by Wilson Follett. New York: Knopf, 1930.

The Poems of Stephen Crane, a critical edition by Joseph Katz. New York: Cooper Square Publishers, 1966.

At Clancy's Wake, in *Last Words*. London: Digby, Long, 1902.

The Blood of the Martyr. Mount Vernon, N.Y.: Peter Pauper Press, [1940]. (A play originally printed in the Sunday magazine of the *New York Press* on April 3, 1898.)

Drama in Cuba, in *The War Dispatches of Stephen Crane,* edited by R. W. Stallman and E. R. Hagemann. New York: New York University Press, 1964.

COLLECTED EDITIONS

A new edition of the complete works of Stephen Crane is now being prepared at the University of Virginia.

The Work of Stephen Crane, edited by Wilson Follett. 12 vols. New York:

Knopf, 1925–27. Recently reprinted in 6 vols., New York: Russell and Russell, 1963.

Stephen Crane: An Omnibus, edited by R. W. Stallman. New York: Knopf, 1952.

Stephen Crane: Uncollected Writings, edited with an introduction by Olov W. Fryckstedt. Uppsala: Almqvist and Wiksell, 1963.

LETTERS

Stephen Crane: Letters, edited by R. W. Stallman and Lillian Gilkes. New York: New York University Press, 1960.

CURRENT AMERICAN REPRINTS

A great many paperback editions of *The Red Badge of Courage* are available, including one published by the New American Library (Signet edition) edited by R. W. Stallman ($.50), one by Dell ($.50) with an introduction by Ralph Ellison, and one by Bobbs-Merrill in the Library of Literature series with an introduction by Frederick C. Crews containing material on the battle of Chancellorsville ($1.25). *The Red Badge of Courage and Selected Prose and Poetry*, edited by William M. Gibson (Holt, Rinehart, and Winston, $1.50), offers, besides *The Red Badge* and four vignettes with a war interest, some of Crane's best work: *Maggie*, "The Men in the Storm," "The Open Boat," "The Bride Comes to Yellow Sky," "The Monster," "The Blue Hotel," and a few poems. Excellent selections are also found in *Stephen Crane: Stories and Tales*, edited by R. W. Stallman (Vintage, $1.45); *Great Short Works of Stephen Crane*, with an introduction by James B. Colvert (Harper-Row, $.95); and *The Red Badge of Courage and Other Writings*, edited by Richard Chase (Houghton Mifflin Riverside edition, $1.25). The Norton critical edition of *The Red Badge of Courage*, edited by S. Bradley ($1.95), introduces the reader to a wide range of interpretations, including essays by H. G. Wells, Joseph Conrad, and Ford Madox Ford. *The Red Badge of Courage: Text and Criticism*, edited by Richard Lettis (Harcourt, Brace and World, $2.45), is a useful textbook.

Bibliography

A new bibliography is being prepared by R. W. Stallman for Iowa State University Press. Since 1963 Syracuse University has issued an annual Crane bibliography in *Thoth*.

Williams, Ames W., and Vincent Starrett. *Stephen Crane: A Bibliography*. Glendale, Calif.: John Valentine, 1948.

Biographies

Beer, Thomas. *Stephen Crane*. New York: Knopf, 1923.

Berryman, John. *Stephen Crane*. New York: William Sloane Associates, 1950. Reprinted in 1962 as a Meridian paperback with an additional preface.

Gilkes, Lillian. *Cora Crane*. Bloomington: Indiana University Press, 1960. (Although centered on Cora, this contains much information on the life of the couple in England.)

Raymond, Thomas L. *Stephen Crane*. Newark, N.J.: Carteret Book Club, 1923.

Stallman, R. W. *Stephen Crane*. New York: Braziller, 1968.

Critical Studies

Bassan, Maurice. "Crane, Townsend, and Realism of a Good Kind," *Proceedings of the New Jersey Historical Society*, 82:128–35 (April 1964).

Berryman, John. "The Red Badge of Courage," in *The American Novel*, edited by Wallace Stegner. New York: Basic Books, 1965.

Berthoff, Warner. *The Ferment of Realism: American Literature 1884–1919*. New York: Free Press, 1965.

Cady, Edwin H. *Stephen Crane*. New York: Twayne, 1962.

Colvert, James B. "The Origins of Stephen Crane's Literary Creed," *University of Texas Studies in English*, 34:179–88 (1955).

Ellison, Ralph. Introduction to *The Red Badge of Courage*. New York: Dell, 1960. Reprinted in *Shadow and Act*. New York: Random House, 1964.

Geismar, Maxwell. *Rebels and Ancestors*. Boston: Houghton Mifflin, 1953.

Gibson, Donald B. *The Fiction of Stephen Crane*. Carbondale: Southern Illinois University Press, 1968.

Gordan, John D. "*The Ghost* at Brede Place," *Bulletin of the New York Public Library*, 56:591–96 (December 1952).

Greenfield, Stanley B. "The Unmistakable Stephen Crane," *PMLA*, 73:562–72 (December 1958).

Gullason, Thomas. "Stephen Crane's Private War on Yellow Journalism," *Huntington Library Quarterly*, 22:200–8 (May 1959).

Hoffman, D. G. *The Poetry of Stephen Crane*. New York: Columbia University Press, 1957.

________. "Stephen Crane's Last Novel," *Bulletin of the New York Public Library*, 64:337–43 (June 1960).

Katz, Joseph. "'The Blue Battalions' and the Uses of Experience," *Studia Neophilogica*, 38:107–16 (1966).

________, ed. *Stephen Crane Newsletter*, Fall 1966 to date.

Kazin, Alfred. "American Fin de Siècle," in *On Native Grounds*. New York: Reynal and Hitchcock, 1942.

Lytle, Andrew. " 'The Open Boat': A Pagan Tale," in *The Hero with the Private Parts*. Baton Rouge: Louisiana State University Press, 1966.

Martin, Jay. *Harvests of Change: American Literature, 1865–1914*. Englewood Cliffs, N.J.: Prentice-Hall, 1967.

Modern Fiction Studies, 5:199–291 (Autumn 1959). (Essays on Crane by Thomas A. Gullason, Robert F. Gleckner, Peter Buitenhuis, James B. Colvert, R. W. Stallman, Hugh Maclean, Eric Solomon, James T. Cox; also contains a good selective bibliography.)

Nelson, Harland S. "Stephen Crane's Achievement as a Poet," *University of Texas Studies in Literature and Language*, 4:564–82 (Winter 1963).

Ross, Lillian. *Picture*. London: Penguin Books, 1962. Reprinted from the *New Yorker*, May–June 1952. (An account of the filming of *The Red Badge of Courage* for MGM under the direction of John Huston.)

Schneider, Robert W. *Five Novelists of the Progressive Era*. New York: Columbia University Press, 1965.

Solomon, Eric. *Stephen Crane: From Parody to Realism*. Cambridge, Mass.: Harvard University Press, 1966.

Vasilievskaya, O. B. *The Work of Stephen Crane*. Moscow: Nayka Editions, 1967. (A critical study in Russian.)

Walcutt, Charles Child. *American Literary Naturalism, a Divided Stream*. Minneapolis: University of Minnesota Press, 1956.

Weisenberger, Bernard. "The Red Badge of Courage," in Charles Shapiro, ed., *Twelve Original Essays on Great American Novels*. Detroit: Wayne State University Press, 1958.

Weiss, Daniel. "The Red Badge of Courage," *Psychoanalytic Review*, 52:32–52 (Summer 1965), 52:130–54 (Fall 1965).

Westbrook, Max. "Stephen Crane's Poetry: Perspective and Arrogance," *Bucknell Review*, 11:23–34 (December 1963).

Ziff, Larzer. *The American 1890s*. New York: The Viking Press, 1966.

STIRLING COUNTY LIBRARY
STIRLING DISTRICT LIBRARY